Trees
of the Bible

Illustrated by Vic Mitchell

Little Lions

LION PUBLISHING

Acacia

The acacia is one of the few trees
which grows in the bare desert of
Sinai. Acacia wood was used to
make the 'ark', the Israelites'
Covenant Box which held the
copies of the laws God gave to
Moses.

Cedar

The giant cedar tree used to grow in great forests in Lebanon. It has a warm red wood which lasts well. King Solomon bought cedar-wood to make beautiful carved panels for his temple and his palace.

Fir and pine

The evergreen fir and pine
trees grew on the mountains
and hills of Israel. They were
used to make ships' decks,
musical instruments and
parts of the temple in
Jerusalem.

Myrtle

The myrtle is an evergreen tree. It
has sweet-smelling leaves and
white flowers which are used for
perfume.

Oak

In Israel there are many kinds of
oak tree. Some of them are
evergreen. They grow for many
years and become very strong trees.
Oak was used for oars and for
carved statues.

Poplar

It was probably a kind of poplar tree that the Jewish exiles found in Babylon. They sat down by the river beside the trees and wept because they were homesick. The white poplar gives very thick shade under its leaves.

Terebinth

The terebinth is a low, wide-spreading tree. It is found in warm, dry, hilly places in Israel.

Almond

The almond was the first fruit-tree to blossom in Israel. It sometimes came into flower in January. It was a favourite food and also gave almond oil.

Gourd

A gourd grew up rapidly to shade the prophet Jonah from the hot sun. This may have been the fast-growing castor-oil bush.

Fig and sycomore fig

The fig was an important fruit in Bible times. Fig-trees carry fruit about ten months in every year. The fig leaves are big and are useful for wrapping up food. Dried fig-cakes made good food for a journey.

It was a sycomore fig-tree that little Zacchaeus climbed to get a better view of Jesus.

Olive

Olive berries were very important as fruit. They were picked in November. Some were pickled for eating; most were pressed to make olive oil. Olive oil was used for cooking, to light lamps and to soothe the skin. Olive-trees can grow to be hundreds of years old. Their wood can be carved and polished, as it was in Solomon's temple.

Pomegranate

The pomegranate is a big shrub
with deep green leaves and scarlet
flowers. It has yellowy-brown fruit,
about the size of an orange. The
fruit has a hard skin, but is juicy
and full of seeds. It is good to eat.

Palm (date)

The date palm is a tall, straight
tree, with a huge clump of leaves
at the top. Amongst the leaves are
clusters of dates. People waved
palm leaves when Jesus rode into
Jerusalem in triumph.

Vine

The fruit of the vine is the grape.
When Moses sent spies into the
promised land they brought back
great clusters of grapes to show
how rich the land was.

Vines were planted in rows on
the hillsides to catch the sun.
They were cut back each spring to
make them more fruitful. When
the grapes were getting ripe, the
owner kept guard over them.

At harvest they were picked.
Some were eaten or made into
raisin-cakes. But most were
trodden to make wine. The wine
was stored in skins or pots.

Jesus often used the vine as a
picture in his stories. He said he
was like a vine, and his followers
like branches.

You can read about these trees in the Bible. This is where you can find them:

Acacia	Exodus 25:1-30
Cedar	1 Kings 6:1, 15 – 7:12
Fir and pine	Ezekiel 27:1-5
Myrtle	Nehemiah 8:13-18
Oak	2 Samuel 18:6-17
Poplar	Genesis 30:25-43
Almond	Numbers 17:1-11
Fig and sycomore fig	Luke 19:1-10
Gourd	Jonah 4
Olive	1 Kings 6:23-33
Palm	John 12:12-19
Pomegranate	Numbers 13
Vine	Numbers 13; John 15:1-10

This book has been adapted from **The Lion Encyclopedia of the Bible** – 320 pages of reference material in full colour on Bible people, places, facts and background.

Lion Publishing
121 High Street, Berkhamsted, Herts, England

First edition 1978
International Standard Book Number 0 85648 111 4

Printed in Britain by Balding and Mansell, Wisbech, Cambs